Lyrics from the Heart

Including Goodbye Songs From The Heart

JB Heart

Lyrics From The Heart
Including Goodbye Songs From The Heart
by J.B. Heart

Copyright © 2014 J.B. Heart

Published by Cool Breeze Writers and Publishers
www.CoolBreezePublishing.com

Softcover: ISBN 978-0-9915741-8-6

Cover and interior design by Kathryn Marcellino
of MarcellinoDesign.com

Printed in the United States of America

Preface

Hello this is JB.

I am mostly known for my penmanship as a romance novelist, but I have a passion for writing lyrics. I put together a few of my favorites for you and hope you enjoy them as much as I enjoyed writing them. My hope is that someone can take these romantic lyrics and make great love songs out of them by adding a great voice, great music and a heart of their own to them!

Table of Contents

"God Needed An Angel" was probably the first attempt I made at serious song writing. It came from my heart, more so than any other song that I have written. A wonderful young singer, song writer himself from New Zealand named Jono Heaps, immediately saw the potential for this song, made a few lyric changes so it would fit to music and made a phenomenal recording for me. It was written about a blind friend of mine who passed away October 2, 2009. Bruce helped me regain my passion for writing by teaching me how to use a speech program on the computer after losing my own sight. He fell in love with a zany little pink flamingo named Fitz that I write about in my children's books and cried at my heart wrenching suspense novel *The Silent Fear.* He was instrumental in choosing my pen name, one because he said I wrote from the heart, and two, it was his mother's maiden name.

God Needed An Angel

How could you leave me, when things were so good?
I would ask God one question, if I could. Why?
It took me a lifetime to find you and now you are gone
I am all alone again. Why did things go wrong? And I cry.

Turn around; turn around come back for me.
My heart is breaking. Can't you see?
We were meant to be together, so the song went,
But God needed an angel and for you he sent.
But what about me?

We had so much laughter on a date in the rain,
But now that you have left me. I am filled with anger and pain.
Why?
Our friendship was cut short but it was so strong,
Each time I turn on the radio, they are playing our song and I cry.

Turn around. Turn around. Come back for me.
My heart is breaking. Can't you see?
We were meant to be together, so the song went,
But God needed an angel and for you he sent.
But what about me?

You have left me behind, and I am all alone.
I reach out to call you, but you're not on the phone.
Why my life is so empty, I'll never understand.
Why didn't you reach out and ask for my hand? Now I cry.

Turn around. Turn around. Come back for me.
My heart is breaking. Can't you see?
We were meant to be together, so the song went,
But God needed an angel and for you he sent.
But what about me?

"Dreamer Of Dreams" came to me in the summer of 2013. Through a blind community chat site that I am the president of called Blindcafe.net, I met Kevin Pugh, another singer, song writer. I wanted to write something he could sing. Once again, after my initial words, Kevin did some re-writing to make the words fit to music, and we came up with this very beautiful inspired love song about two people who never met but dreamed of being in Venice together.

Dreamer Of Dreams

I'm a dreamer of dreams.
I was waiting for my dream to come true.
On a hot summer night
I'd get lost in dreams of you.
And though we'd never touched
We loved our way around the world.
Deep within my heart I knew
Some day you'd be my girl.

I'm the dreamer of dreams,
Dreaming 'bout you.
I'm the dreamer of dreams,
Dreaming the whole day through.
I'm the dreamer of dreams.
I'm the dreamer of dreams,
Dreaming 'bout you.

I've never looked in your eyes,
But I saw the depth of your soul.
At the sound of your voice,
I lost all control.
We sailed to the islands,
Crossed the seven seas,
Made love in Venice.
We were oh so wild and free.

I'm the dreamer of dreams,
Dreaming 'bout you.
I'm the dreamer of dreams,
Dreaming the whole day through.
I'm the dreamer of dreams.
I'm the dreamer of dreams,
Dreaming 'bout you.
We sipped wine making memories,

At a quiet table for two,
Shared a kissed in the moonlight,
And danced the whole night through.

You once were my dream,
Just a voice on the phone,
But now you're here to love me,
And you're the sweetest dream I've known.

I'm the dreamer of dreams,
Dreaming 'bout you.
I'm the dreamer of dreams,
Dreaming the whole day through.
I'm the dreamer of dreams.
I'm the dreamer of dreams,
Still dreaming 'bout you.

"Caribbean Cabaret" was written about a night on my honeymoon. My husband and I took a cruise on a ship called the Majestic, which sailed to the Abacus Islands in the Bahamas. Again the romantic comes out in me as I remember the cool breeze blowing and dancing under the moonlight on the beach, while the band played Matilda. The Tiki lights and the moon were the only things lighting up the sky, and it made me think of Fred Astaire and Ginger Rogers in an old black and white movie, dancing a waltz, rendezvousing on a Caribbean Island.

Caribbean Cabaret

Moonlight rendezvous and a tropical breeze,
Coconuts sway in the island trees.
The steel drums are playing
And our bodies are swaying
To the music of the Caribbean cabaret.

We're like two ships out to sea
That left land just to flee
To this paradise for two.
Let's tango, me and you
To the music of the Caribbean cabaret.

The piano keys are sweet,
The warm sand is beneath our feet,
The moonlight is serenading,
While Matilda is playing,
To the music of the Caribbean cabaret.

Miss Emily's Blue Bee Bar
From here is not that far.
You can laugh and have fun
And drink coconut rum
To the music of the Caribbean cabaret.

The sun is coming up,
And we leave this rendezvous behind.
I can't wait for this movie to rewind,
So once again we can be together,
Dancing here forever
To the music of the Caribbean cabaret.

"Baby You're A Sin" was written on a whim. It was another song that Jono my friend from New Zealand saw and immediately got an idea for music. I loved the jazzy sound he put to this one. I wrote an extra bridge after he had recorded it and so it was never finished.

Baby You're A Sin

You walked into my life today,
And baby, it's where I want you to stay.
I opened up my heart to you and let you in,
Even though baby, I know you're a sin. (You're a sin.)

Your hair, your eyes, your smile so sweet.
When you touch me, I can feel the heat.
You hooked me fast and reeled me in,
Even though baby, I know you're a sin.

My hearts beating for you with desire,
Your lips on mine, oo oo feel the fire.
I don't know what to do,
Or where to begin,
Because for me baby, you're a sin.

I don't know where this is gonna go.
Let's take it easy, nice and slow.
Let's risk it all and play to win,
Even though baby, I know you're a sin.
Take my hand baby, lead the way.
Tomorrow morning's a brand new day.
Turn those lights down so there nice and dim,
Oo oo baby you are such a sin.

I love the way you make me feel.
Together we could be the real deal.
I don't care what people say. You're under my skin
Even though baby, I know you're a sin.

"Finally Over You" is not particularly romantic but it goes very deep, and I imagined the music to be quite dark, just like the person I wrote the song for. It was written for a friend of mine who was going through a rough time in his marriage and knew he needed to get out before it turned fatal. I was so scared for both of them after a fight they had one night that the only way to get the pictures out of my mind was to write down the account of what happened that night.

Finally Over You

I Just realized in my mind, that I'm finally over you,
It's the last straw.
It's the last straw.
Your tears don't hurt me any more.
It's become too intense, and I've lost myself.
Our loves turned into hurt and we just say things,
Say things until I just feel like dirt.

You broke me, broke me in two.
It's not about us. It's always just been about you.
The end is here, after all these years.
We used to be one.
Can't you see, oh baby. Can't you see that we are done?
My head is spinning out of control.
I'm loosing myself and I'm loosing my soul.
I need to breathe. I need the strength to leave.

I cannot stay. I just gotta go away.
I've cried enough tears. I've felt enough pain.
Do we have to keep doing this again and again?
The anger that I feel inside is starting to define
Dark thoughts within my mind.

I don't know what happened to our forever.
Was it ever right?
Every time we get together
All we do is fight.
I Just realized that I'm finally over you.
It's the last straw.
Your tears don't hurt me any more.

"**Baby Blues**" is one of my favorite songs. I have heard some music by BB King that would be perfect for these lyrics. Now if only I could get him to sing them ☺. I would love for him to put his bluesy music and his raspy voice to these lyrics. It's about two kids taking off together and getting hitched just like in the movie Bonnie and Clyde.

Baby Blues

I was trapped by your charms.
Now I wanna live wrapped in your arms
Cause your love makes me crazy
And baby we've got nothing to lose.
I've got the wheel in my hand and this little gold band.
Baby, baby, I love your baby blues.

This old road ain't been easy. It's been so cold and so breezy,
but my heart's been on fire with a burning desire,
and baby we've got nothing to lose.
Tonight, there's a sweet smell in the air.
It's that love we're gonna share.
Baby, baby, I love your baby blues.

When the sun peeks through the morning skies,
I thank God for those baby blue eyes.
There's a fire in my soul and it burns out of control.
You know baby we've got nothing to lose.
I've got the wheel in my hand and a little gold band.
Baby, baby, I love your baby blues.
Baby, baby, I love your baby blues.

"Get To Me" reflects on Florida's lazy, hazy, summer days. Sometimes as I sit here at my computer. I dream about a Knight in Shining Armor whisking me away. I picture us riding bareback along the beach on a beautiful white horse. These lyrics not only reflect the romantic novelist in me but the actress inside of me that is dying to escape.

Get To Me

It's a hot Florida afternoon and the sun's blazing.
Lying here with thoughts of you making me hazy.
Dreaming about how you are driving me crazy.
Your love for me is more than amazing,

Baby, your love ignites me, excites me.
You've got to get to me, fight for me.
I need to breathe. I've got to leave.
Baby, baby, you've got to get to me.
It's so intense with us. I cannot wait.
It's our destiny. It's our fate.
When I'm not with you my heart aches and I feel pain.
Oh yeah, you've got to get to me before it rains.

My heart's on fire waiting for you.
I don't care what you have to do.
Spread your wings set me free.
Just come on and get to me.

Baby, your love ignites me, excites me.
You've got to get to me, fight for me.
I need to breathe. I've got to leave.
Baby, baby, you've got to get to me.
It's so intense with us. I cannot wait.
It's our destiny. It's our fate.
When I'm not with you my heart aches and I feel pain.
Oh yeah, you've got to get to me before it rains.

Baby, your love ignites me, excites me.
You've got to get to me, fight for me.
I need to breathe. I've got to leave.
Baby, baby, you've got to get to me.
Baby, baby, you've got to get to me.

"Corner For Two" is about how everything is made for two. Tables in quiet corners in restaurants, sports cars made for two, even great big beds are made for two, but what do you do when you are now only one?

Corner For Two

In a corner there's a table for two.
I am there but where are you?
Now that you're gone and I'm all alone
Is this how it's going to be?

The moon is shining bright.
It's a beautiful night.
Lovers holding hands
While I walk alone along the sand.

How do I cover up this pain inside my heart?
I'm so alone now since we've been apart.
I don't know what to do.
All I know is, there's no me without you.

There's a bed made for two.
I'm lying here where are you?
The telephone rings
But I know it's not you
Because that perfect picture
With the sky so blue
Is a picture of heaven with an angels view.

How do I cover up this pain inside my heart?
I'm so alone now since we've been apart.
I don't know what to do.
All I know is, there's no me without you.

I'm driving in a car built for two
On a lonely highway. Where are you?
It's like the sun without the glare
As the wind races through my hair.

I'm trying to be really strong
But all I'm doing is holding on.
Everything in this world is made for two
And I am only one without you.

How do I cover up this pain inside my heart?
I'm so alone now since we've been apart.
I don't know what to do.
All I know is, there's no me without you.

Tonight I'm gonna open a bottle of sweet red wine
And remember how your lips felt on mine.
I'm gonna go back
And remember that time
When I was yours
And you were mine.
I feel like a bird without a song.
The worlds standing still and everything is wrong.

How do I cover up this pain inside my heart?
I'm so alone now since we've been apart.
I don't know what to do.
All I know is, there's no me without you.

"Romance At A Glance." I thought about a scene from lady and the tramp when I wrote these words. I loved the scene were they were sucking on a spaghetti strand together. I think I had a combination of that music and Lady in Red in mind when I got inspired to write the lyrics to this one.

Romance At A Glance

All it took when I saw you, was one, quick glance.
And then you came over, and you asked, me to dance.
We sat down, at a table, meant just for two.
These feelings, that I'm feeling, inside me, are new.

Your hand behind my head pulled me closer in
And everything, I was thinking, about you was a sin.
Our lips touched each others, across the glass of wine.
And we kissed each other for the very first time.
Your fingers, they touched mine, as you reached for my hand.
And time still like an hour glass of sand.

The first thing I thought of was this love at first sight?
Is this feeling I'm feeling gonna last for more than night?
I wanted to tell you those three little words,
But knew that my secret was just for the birds.
And now I'm left with this feeling that I've never felt before,
And a glance from your eyes that I want forever more.

The moonlight is shining as we stroll along.
And in the distance, we can hear that now familiar song,
The one they were playing when you asked me to dance.
We stopped for a moment and your lips kissed mine.
It reminded me of that sweet glass of wine.
My heart began to fill with thoughts of romance,
And it all started with that one little glance.

The first thing I thought of was this love at first sight?
Is this feeling that I'm feeling gonna last for more than one
night?
I wanted to tell you those three little words,
But I knew that my secret was just for the birds.
And now I'm left with this feeling that I've never felt before.

Is this feeling that I'm feeling gonna last for more than one night?

Thoughts of you fill me with passion and desire.
My heart aches for you like a fresh burning fire.
When our body's first embrace and loneliness leaves me without a trace,
I'll always remember this romance at a glance,
And the way that you held me when you asked me to dance.

The first thing I will think of, is this love at first sight?
Is this feeling I'm feeling gonna last for more than tonight?
I wanted to tell you those three little words,
But knew that my secret was just for the birds.
So I'm left with this feeling that I've never felt before,
And a glance from your eyes that I want forever more.

And I want it to last forever more.

A song simply named "**Time.**" These lyrics are recent, and they are in a time in my life when I am really challenging myself in many new areas and definitely doing things outside of the box for me. I have new romance novels on the way, new children's books, *Lyrics from the Heart*, and I have even tried my hand at singing!

Time

You turned my head and I looked your way.
You said I love you and I want you to stay.
My arms have been waiting a long, long time
For you to fall into and be mine.
You asked me a question and that's all it took.
It was like a page taken from a romance book.
You gambled and you played to win.
Then said you loved me and you moved right in.

You reached right in and you stole my heart.
You knew you had me from the very start.
You reeled me in like a fish on a hook.
You knew what to say; you knew what it took.
You said you loved me and you moved right in.
I hear your voice and then once again
You say that you love me and drive me insane.
Oh yeah babe, you make me feel so wild and free.

Oh yeah babe, you make me feel so wild and free.

I feel your passion and your fire.
My heart it aches for you with desire.
I'm glad you found me come hold me tight.
And make love to me all through the night.
You drive me crazy lady. Can't you see?
Oh yeah lady, you make me feel so wild and free.

Oh yeah babe, you make me feel so wild and free.

You say you love my laughter, love my smile
And for me you'd walk a million miles.
You've turned my head and I've looked your way,
But will this last and lady will you stay?
You drive me crazy baby. Can't you see?

Oh yeah babe, you make me feel so wild and free.

Oh yeah babe, you make me feel so wild and free.

"Thinking About You." Being blind, I spend a lot of time on the computer with my friends, and we are always skyping or emailing, and it's amazing how sometimes are computers are in sync with each others. I hear so many people falling in love on the computer that I wrote this song for them.

Thinking About You

I find myself, just thinking about you.
A smile crosses my face while I'm tying my shoe.
I'm sitting at the table singing love songs.
Thoughts of you seem so wrong.
I taste the sweetness of your lips upon mine.
As I take another sip of this glass of wine.

I smile a smile; it's a quarter till three.
I wonder baby are you thinking 'bout me.
You say you're addicted and I know I am too,
Cause just like a junkie, all I do is think about you.
I want your loving, hold me tight.
While I think about you all through the night.

The phone rings; it's early and I know it's you.
Your thinking about me and I'm thinking 'bout you.
Our computers are on; they're both in sync.
Mine wants to know "Baby what does yours think!" (This line
here is said in sexy whimsical voice.)
Are you coming over baby; please say, "Yes."
How did we get caught up in this crazy mess?

I find myself, just thinking about you.
A smile crosses my face while I'm tying my shoe.
Will this work out baby; you say, "Wait and see."
I just want to hear you say it's meant to be.
I want to be with you forever in time.
As I take another sip of this glass of wine.

"First Time." I love this song, I can see Cheryl Crow rock out to this one or Carrie Underwood do her bad girl country style rock to it. It shows a sensual as well as bad girl side of me. My husband laughs at this song as it only took me 15 minutes to write. This is usually how one of my great love scenes in my romance novels start. This is definitely one of my favorites. I would love to rock out to this one myself.

First Time

For the first time in a long time
I feel alive and well.
For the first time in a long time
I don't feel like hell.
I feel like a brand new woman
Cause your love has turned my head.
I feel damn good all over
Hey baby, come on back to bed.

Oh yeah, take me out tonight
And we'll dance the night away.
We'll get drunk and have a party.
Baby, we'll go all the way.

It's the first time in a long time
I'm up off my knees.
For the first time in a long time
I'll do what I damn well please.

Your love has taken me higher
than I've ever been before.
And your love is all I've needed,
all I've been looking for.
So tonight let's make it baby
And get lost in sweet red wine,
Cause for the first time in a long time.
Baby, I'm walking on cloud nine.

"**My Angel Rose**" is a reflection on how strong a memory of a previous love can be. Although in love with someone new, the memory of the old love can be so strong it can destroy whatever is new. Angel Rose could definitely become a character in one of my romance novels.

My Angel Rose

Every time I let her into my mind, things get so cloudy and hard to define.
You're the one that I adore; I really should try harder to forget her I suppose.
It's only for a moment in time, but my heart aches for that girl that used to be mine.
She was my most beautiful, the most perfect, she was my Angel Rose.

Believe me when I tell you darling, I really do try
But she was one in a million, my perfect Angel Rose.
And I can't deny her memory, and I know that makes you cry.
You're the one I'm with though, and you're the one that I choose.

After all these years, I should think only of you, but still her memory slips through.
I know that my guilt shows, and I know that you know.
I wish I could have been true, and only ever have loved you
But there's my beautiful, my perfect, my Angel Rose.

I wish I could forget her and let her memory go,
But she was my most beautiful, the most perfect, she was my Angel Rose.
I try so hard every day not to let my love for her show,
But she was one in a million, my perfect Angel Rose.

"Crazy Love." What can I say about crazy love? It's when those butterflies hit the stomach and you need an exterminator to get rid of them. It's when you miss the person you fell in love with so bad you think your going to burst if you don't hurry up and see them again soon. I hope everyone in life gets to experience this feeling at least once in their lifetime.

Crazy Love

I lay around just being lazy
Cause I'm missing you like crazy.
I hear your sweet voice on the phone
And I'm hit with what I've always known.
Right from the word hello
I should have never let you go
Cause now I'm missing you like crazy.

I wanna be back in your arms tonight.
Your love's perfect for me baby; hold me tight.
I wanna tell the world, I wanna shout it out,
I'm in love with you baby and there ain't no doubt.
Our friends say when were together,
We're happy it's plain to see.
So hurry back baby and get a hold of me
Cause I'm missing you like crazy.

Once your back in my life for sure,
I'm never gonna let you go no more.
Were gonna make it baby; wait and see.
We've always said were meant to be.
Now that I've given you this precious heart
Were never gonna be apart
Cause I don't want to miss you like crazy.

I wanna be back in your arms tonight.
Your love's perfect for me baby; hold me tight.
I wanna tell the world, I wanna shout it out,
I'm in love with you baby and there ain't no doubt.
Our friends say when were together,
We're happy; it's plain to see.
So hurry back baby and get a hold of me
Cause I'm missing you like crazy.

"Where There's A Will," there has to be a way for true love to prevail and claim victory. That is the romantic in me!

Where There's A Will

Tonight's another night,
I'm here all alone
Listening to you softly,
Crying on the phone.
I don't know what else to say
Except where there's a will
There's got to be a way.

My world's a lonely place
But in your arms I would be safe.
Baby girl I promise you,
I'll make all your dreams come true.
I don't know what else to say
Except where there's a will
There's got to be a way.

Chorus:
There's got to be a way.
There's got to be a way
For us to be together
Forever and forever.
I gotta get to you girl.
I gotta have you in my world.
I don't know what else to say.
Where there's a will
There's gotta be a way.

I gotta touch your hair; I gotta see into your eyes.
Wanna be the one who takes you to that high.
I want you to know my heart is true.
And I want to see your face when I say I love you.
I gotta get to you girl.
I gotta have you in my world.

I don't know what else to say.
Where there's a will
There's got to be a way.

Chorus:
There's got to be a way.
There's got to be a way
For us to be together
Forever and forever.
I gotta get to you girl.
I gotta have you in my world.
I don't know what else to say.
Where there's a will
There's gotta be a way.

"Key West" is one of my favorite places to visit. It is like being in the Caribbean only your still on American soil. It's definitely a place of its own, and you can feel the ambiance of the tropics. This is one of my son's favorite songs that I wrote. He even tried to sing his own tune to it!

Key West

Coconut trees and a warm summer breeze
Take me away to the Florida Keys.
Toes in the water, tanning in the sun
Let's soak in this paradise and grab us some fun.

We're alone now baby.
Let's do what we planned,
Make love in the morning, then play in the sand.
Let's drift out to sea on a tropical cruise.

We can party all night. We've got nothing to lose
When the sun goes down and it turns into night.
While the skies still on fire with the Tiki lights
We'll find us a bar and rum or two
And dance in the moonlight just me and you.
We'll sway to the music of Margarittaville
While you slip me your jacket to take off the chill.

Coconut oil and the wind in my hair
Thoughts of back home disappear in the air.
On this paradise isle we don't have a care
Except for the waves and this old rocking chair.
Coconut trees and a warm summer breeze
Take me away to the Florida Keys.

Let's never go home or get back on that plane.
Life in the city will never be the same.
All the noise from the cars and no Tiki bars,
No tropical fruit or an umbrella in my drink,
Or wearing flip flops in flamingo pink,
No coconut trees and no warm summer breeze.
Take me back to the Florida Keys.

"I Wanna Make Love In Venice" is about a sensual person who wants to please their partner in one of the most romantic cities in the world.

I Wanna Make Love In Venice

I wanna make love in Venice with you.
I wanna be everything you need.
I wanna make all your dreams come true.
I want to hear you call my name; I want to hear you plead.

I love you more with every breath I take.
I want to be your harmony.
I hear your voice; I start to shake.
I wanna be your wish come true, your fantasy.

I wanna be the last thing that you see at night.
I want to be your forever more.
I want to be your angel tonight.
I want to be the one you want, the one that you adore.

I wanna be your reason for living.
I wanna hear the beat of your heart.
I wanna be your new beginning,
And never want us to be apart.

All you have to do is close your eyes.
And I will be in front of you.
Pray to heaven baby in the sky
And all our dreams and wishes, he'll make come true.

"**Finally A Love That's Enough.**" A song about how quickly love can come and go. Sometimes, when you finally think you've got it right, and it was meant to be, and it's taken away in a flash. So many people can relate to the words of this song and how heart wrenching this kind of devastation can be. My heart goes out to anyone who has been through a love like this!

Finally A Love That's Enough

Finally I found a love that was enough for me
And baby it came so easily.
Some how... some way... you reached in to my heart
Joining it with yours baby; we'll never part.
Our dreams were the same and the world was right,
Until...until... that one fatal night.

It's "that night" when hearts they get broken
And nights when dreams get shaken.
It's a night when words go unspoken.
It's one of those nights when a life gets taken.

Finally, once again, I'm cold and alone.
And baby, there's no more waiting for the phone.
Some how...some way...I've got to get to you.
I'm going crazy...I don't know what to do.
My dreams were shattered by that fatal night.
Will it ever be...will it ever be...alright?

It's "that night" when hearts they get broken
And nights when dreams get shaken.
It's a night when words go unspoken.
It's one of those nights when a life gets taken.

Finally, the years go by along with the 1000 tears I cried.
Oh baby, why did you have to die?
Somehow...some way...I feel you in my soul
And until we reunite my heart will never be whole.
When we're angels in heaven then all will be right
Until then, until then just hold on to tonight.

When we're angels in heaven then all will be right.
Until then, until then just hold on to tonight.

"How Do You Talk To An Angel." Many people claim they have. I know I have! My Angel is with me every day and is with me in every decision I make especially when it comes to my writing. I know in my heart it will be an Angel that comes along and sings one of my songs. It's meant to be! ☺ This is the third song that Jono and I collaborated on. He changed a few of the words and immediately put music to the words and sent me a recording almost overnight, and I loved it!

How Do You Talk To An Angel

But there's only silence that surrounds
And you are nowhere to be found,
Because how do you talk to an angel?
How do you talk to an angel?

When I'm feeling all alone
And I can't pick up the phone,
How do I talk to my angel?

When I think about the rain
And I'm feeling all this pain,
How do I talk to my angel?

I swear I hear you call my name
And I want you to explain,
But how do I talk to my angel?

I see you in my dreams,
And you're here with me it seems,
But how do I talk to my angel?

Your hands are in my hair
And I feel you in the air,
And I want to talk to my angel.

I want to reach out for your hand
And try to make you understand,
But how do I talk to my angel?

Tonight, tonight, I say my prayers
And pray to God that you are there
So I can talk to my angel.

I ask if I could hear your voice

So once again I could rejoice
And talk to my angel.

I cry so you can hear.
I want you back, I want you near.
How do I talk to my angel?

The way you loved me every day,
There are so many things I want to say
But how do you talk to an angel?

"From The Heart" was written with more emotion than even I thought I was capable of having. The song is very appropriately named as it was definitely written from the heart.

From the Heart

I don't know what I would do in this life without you.
You are all the dreams that I have dreamed
All come true.
If you didn't love me so much, I don't know
What I would do, because now that we are together,
There is no me without you.

God made a shoulder just perfect for my head
And it's yours.
He made your arms to keep me safe
And to hold me through the night.
You walked into my life, and you've made it so right
Because without you, in my life, I don't know what I would do.

I gave you my heart! You rescued me from my pain.
You took my cloudy days! Dried up all my tears,
And brought out the sun again.

If you didn't love me so much,
I don't know what I would do.
Cause baby, if you didn't know,
I'm so in love with you.

I don't know what I would do in this life without you.
I truly believe that you and I were meant to be.
If you didn't love me so much, I don't know
What I would do,
Cause now that we are together,
There is no more me with out you.

There's no more me without you.
There's no more me without you!

"Undying Love." I wrote "Undying Love" for a friend who passed but never finished it. I sent it to my friend Kevin who tinkered with it a little but never really did anything with it either, the unfinished song so to speak. Our chat community, Blindcafe.net had a talent night. Kevin was supposed to sing my song Baby Blues as I had requested he perform that for our charity auction, but he could not find the words for it and so he found "Undying Love," finished the lyrics, and put the music to it. He actually won the competition that night, and we all loved the song, so I included it in this collection. It makes me think of my mom now, looking down on me and watching out for me.

Undying Love

You stepped into my life with a love made just for me,
And I just can't help but wonder why it came so easily.
Wrapped inside your arms I felt like I could fly.
Soaring through the heavens like an eagle in the sky.
I looked inside my heart and found you waiting there
With all the love and laughter,
And all the dreams we used to share.

You always believed in me when I was feeling down,
With just a single word, you could lift me off the ground.
Now I sit alone and cry
Wonderin' how I'll get through the night.
I know you're looking down on me
From somewhere up above,
Sending me your strength and your undying love.

You opened up my soul to help me find a way
Past the pain and tears to the dreams of yesterday.
I look up to heaven and smile a smile for you.
Wishing you were here to help me make it through.

Now I sit alone and cry
Wonderin' how I'll get through the night.
I know you're looking down on me
From somewhere up above,
Sending me your strength and your undying love.

I know you're looking down on me
From somewhere up above,
Sending me your strength and your undying love.

Goodbye's From The Heart

The year 2014 has not been a kind year to me. I suffered losses in my life that were more devastating to me than the loss of my sight, one being my wonderful mother, who passed away April 30th. C.O.P.D and loss of memory is a dreadful disease both for the person dying from it and the family members watching their loved one's living through it.

For me it was extra hard as half the time I was in fear that my mom would hurt herself, and I would not be able to help her in time. I know my mom would want me to acknowledge my husband and his mom as without them, I could not have survived her passing and neither could she have. My husband was her rock and should be commended for the wonderful and compassionate aid he gave to my mom who was very scared to leave this world. Thanks, Rick ☺.

For this reason, I have added a few extra songs to my collection of lyrics and a couple of goodbye poems that were truly written from the heart. The next few pages are for the people who brought love and laughter to my life and that have now left a hole along with much sadness and sorrow. Hopefully I've put together words that will relate and maybe help someone else who is hurting as much as I am today.

"A Window Into Her Heart." This poem was inspired by the loss of another dear friend. I believe God puts people in your life at certain times for certain reasons. Some of the people stay forever and some are just there to help you through a difficult time. This poem was about one of those times for me.

My husband tells me all the time that I have a huge, giving heart, and it is taken advantage of time and again. He tries to protect my heart whenever he can, but there are just some people who are more determined than others to break it. He vows that he will be by my side forever as he is the one and only. He has not only looked into the window of my heart, but he has looked into my soul and believes that he is a lucky man, because my true love lies with him!

The Window Into Her Heart

I let him see through the window into my heart.
It's a place now that no one else will see.
I'm now forever cautious of love and men that prey.
And those 3 words for some that are so easy to say.

I love butterflies, ice cream and muffins with jam.
I tell silly jokes about ducks and putting bills on their beaks,
And say funny words like "darn it," but I don't say "damn."
It's all those little things that add up and make me unique.

He sensed the sweetness of me coming from within,
And my love and laughter he adored.
He chased me and my heart; he couldn't wait to win.
And my passion for life left him wanting more.

He said I brought out the best in him right from the start;
Said our friendship was a keeper from the moment that we met,
So I opened the window and let him into my heart,
Then suddenly he changed and he began having regrets.

He didn't want to hurt me or to break my heart,
And my friendship was the best that he'd ever known.
And even when someone hurts me I don't just depart.
It's a friendship that before he'd never been shown.

My friends say he didn't deserve my love; that is for sure.
They knew from the start he was telling me lies.
He's left me so empty so hurt and even more insecure,
And for as long as he lives he will hear my heart's cries.

My passion and the flame inside me are gone,
But time heals all wounds; that's what all my friends say.
So I smile, close the window to my heart and go on, and
Pray that his memory fades a little more with each passing day.

"**Adios Amigo.**" This song was written in my hot tub. I was relaxing with my husband and son and suddenly began singing them the words. They started laughing hysterically and made me promise to remember the words once we got out of the tub as they both loved the lyrics. I noticed each of them singing the words around the house the next day and wondered, hmmm, maybe the country music awards some day, LOL!

I have to give an extra thanks to Kathryn Marcellino of Marcellino Design for the way she placed this song on the page. You will see the guy's parts are indented. I hope you enjoy this fun song!

Adios Amigo

I'm waiting here for you to pick me up.
I love you, like I love your Chevy truck.
I'm tired of hearing you sing the same old song.
I've waited for you just a little too darn long.
So honey you had better be on your way,
Or it's Adios Amigo and have a nice day.

    Since when did you start liking my Chevy truck?
    Oh, Honey, was it when you ran out of luck?
    I've been waiting on you to make up your mind,
    But, Honey, believe me when I say I know your kind.
    You ain't ready to settle down and stay,
    And so Adios Amiga and have a nice day.

Listen here, Cowboy, I've been waiting on you.
Those rumors you've been hearing, they ain't true.
You need to be a coming round my front door,
Or you and me baby, we ain't gonna be no more.
You need to promise me that your always gonna stay
Or it's Adios Amigo and have a nice day.

    You may be sexy, sweet and pure,
    And think you've hooked me; that's for sure.
    I know that I've been calling for some time,
    And thought that you girl were all mine
    But if you don't hurry and change your ways,
    It's Adios Amiga and have a nice day.

Okay, Cowboy, then let's get hitched.
I'm tired of hearing you whine and bitch.
It's time for you to come pick me up.
I love you like I love your Chevy truck.
I'm tired of hearing you sing the same old song.
I've waited for you just a little too darn long.

So honey you had better be on your way
Or it's Adios Amigo and have a nice day.

So honey you had better be on your way
Or it's Adios Amigo and have a nice day.

I Know I Made Mistakes

I know I made mistakes,
Said things I shouldn't have.
How do you take them back?
How do I make you see
That you belong with me?

How do I erase you from my mind,
And make you a distant memory?
Right now the hurt is still brand new,
And all my thoughts are still of you.

I sit alone in silence.
There's no laughter, no love.
I got so lost in you,
And I need to find myself.
Now I don't know what to do.

In time I'll erase you from my mind,
And you'll become just a memory.
But for now the hurt is still brand new
And all my thoughts are still of you.

Once your dreams were my dreams
To live and love on a beach,
To spend our lives together.
Why did things go so wrong?
Now it's all so out of reach.

So in time I'll erase you from my mind,
And you'll become just a memory,
But for now the hurt is still brand new,
And all my thoughts are still of you.

You made me reach for the skies
Then shattered all our dreams.
Every promise was just a lie.
And then you turned so cold and mean.
So In time I'll erase you from my mind,
And you'll become just a memory.
But for now the hurt is still brand new,
And all my thoughts are still of you.

But for now the hurt is still brand new,
And all my thoughts are still of you.

"I Still Feel You." This song was the hardest to write of all, yet the words came the easiest. It is the last song after a year of putting *Lyrics From The Heart* together. I'm sad that a project that started out so beautiful ended in so much pain. I am going to return to writing my novels and children's books. You can find them at JBHeart.net.

I Still Feel You

I still feel you with me.
I know I made mistakes.
Huh! We've all done that before
I know that I let you down
But you . . . you shattered all our dreams
With your promises and your lies,
And even though it's over,
I still feel you with me
Cause baby, I still love you,
And you'll always be a part of me. Oh woe.

I can't think straight.
Baby, I can't sleep at night.
You want me to erase you from my heart,
But I can't do that. Oh no.
Cause when I close my eyes,
I still see you and feel you,
And want that crazy love that we once had,
Cause baby, I still love you,
And you'll always be a part of me. Oh woe.

Dreams are for dreamers.
Huh! And wishes are for the stars.
You promised me forever,
And now I don't even know who you are,
And even though it's over,
I still feel you with me,
Cause baby, I still love you
And you'll always be a part of me. Oh woe.

And even though it's over,
I still feel you with me,
Cause baby, I still love you
And you'll always be a part of me. Oh woe.

Goodbye Song from the Heart

I sit at my keyboard writing my songs,
Waiting for the right words to come along.
Thoughts of you enter my mind.
I wonder what you're doing,
And how you're spending your time.
My heart it's still breaking, and I cry every day,
Cause you left me alone; You just couldn't stay.

And I ask the good Lord how could this be?
Why is my mother not here with me?
I'm left in darkness with all of this pain,
And just the sound of my keyboard and the pouring rain.

I write songs about angels and heaven above.
I'm an author of books all about love.
Nothing can prepare you for the day of repent,
Then came the words God needed an angel and for you he sent.
And I die a little more inside me today,
Cause you left me alone; you just couldn't stay.

And I ask the good Lord
How could this be?
Why is my mother not here with me?
I'm left in darkness with all of this pain,
And just the sound of my keyboard and the pouring rain.

Why do we suffer on this earth where we live?
Why can't we be generous, kind and forgive?
Our mothers and fathers and loved ones we lose,
Some to senseless crimes that they definitely don't choose,
Others to illness as we look on while they suffer.
It's supposed to make us strong and somehow tougher,
But for me I just want love and I cry harder today.
Cause you left me alone; you just couldn't stay.

And I ask the good Lord
How could this be?
Why is my mother not here with me?
I'm left in darkness with all of this pain,
And just the sound of my keyboard and the pouring rain.

I love you, mom.

Always,
JB

www.ingramcontent.com/pod-product-compliance
Lightning Source LLC
Chambersburg PA
CBHW071633040426
42452CB00009B/1608